Seashores

Anita Ganeri

Raintree

www.raintreepublishers.co.uk
Visit our website to find out more information about Raintree books.

To order:
☎ Phone 0845 6044371
🖷 Fax +44 (0) 1865 312263
🖳 Email myorders@capstonepub.co.uk

Customers from outside the UK please telephone +44 1865 312262

Raintree is an imprint of Capstone Global Library Limited, a company incorporated in England and Wales having its registered office at 7 Pilgrim Street, London, EC4V 6LB – Registered company number: 6695582

"Raintree" is a registered trademark of Pearson Education Limited, under licence to Capstone Global Library Limited

Edited by Charlotte Guillain, Nancy Dickmann, and Catherine Veitch
Designed by Joanna Hinton-Malivoire
Picture research by Elizabeth Alexander and Ruth Blair
Original illustrations © Capstone Global Library
Original illustrations by Joanna Hinton-Malivoire (p. 28)
Production by Victoria Fitzgerald
Originated by Capstone Global Library Ltd
Printed and bound in China by Leo Paper Products

ISBN 978 0 431 17245 3
14 13 12 11 10
10 9 8 7 6 5 4 3 2 1

British Library Cataloguing in Publication Data
Ganeri, Anita.
Seashores. -- (Nature trails)
577.6'99-dc22

Acknowledgements
We would like to thank the following for permission to reproduce photographs: Alamy pp. **16** (© tbkmedia.de), **27** (© redsnapper); Corbis pp. **4-5** (© John Harper), **7** (© Lee Frost/ Robert Harding World Imagery), **6** (© Ashley Cooper), **8** (© Radius Images), **22** (© Roger Tidman), **26** (© Roger Hutchings); FLPA pp. **15** (© D P Wilson), **25** (© ImageBroker); iStockphoto pp **12** (© Iain Sarjeant); **14, 20, 23** (© Sophie Demange), **29 left** (© Merlin Farwell), **21 right** (© chris beddoe); Photolibrary pp. **9** (White), **10** (Photononstop), **18** (OSF/Paul Kay), **24** (Naill Benvie/Oxford Scientific); Shutterstock pp **29 right** (© Jerome Whittingham), **21 left** (© nito).

Cover photograph of Durdle Door, Lulworth Cove Bay reproduced with permission of Corbis (© Grand Tour).

The publisher would like to thank Emma Shambrook for her assistance in the preparation of this book.

Every effort has been made to contact copyright holders of material reproduced in this book. Any omissions will be rectified in subsequent printings if notice is given to the publisher.

All the internet addresses (URLs) given in this book were valid at the time of going to press. However, due to the dynamic nature of the Internet, some addresses may have changed or ceased to exist since publication. While the author and publishers regret any inconvenience this may cause readers, no responsibility for any such changes can be accepted by either the author or the publishers.

Contents

Any words appearing in the text in bold, **like this**, are explained in the glossary.

What is a seashore?

A seashore is where the sea meets the land. Britain is made up of islands with sea all around them. This means that there are plenty of seashores for you to explore.

A seashore is a type of **habitat**. A habitat is a place where plants and animals live. Many different plants and animals live along the seashores around Britain.

In this book, the Signpost boxes ask you to find out about more animals and plants. Ask an adult to help you find information in books at school, in the library, or on the Internet.

Rocky and sandy

There are two main types of seashore: rocky and sandy. Rocky seashores are covered in pebbles and rocks that break away from the cliffs. Seashore plants cling to the rocks. Animals hide in cracks in the rocks and in rock pools.

rocky seashore

Many animals live buried underneath the sand.

Sandy seashores are covered in sand. Sand is made up of tiny pieces of rock and broken-up seashells. Sometimes the wind blows the sand into hills, called **sand dunes**.

Changing tides

Every day, the seashore **habitat** changes from wet to dry and back again. This is because of the **tides**. Twice a day, at high tide, the sea flows on to the shore. It covers the rocks or sand.

When the tide comes in, it can cut you off from the land. Make sure you know the tide times.

Twice a day, at low tide, the sea flows back out again. It uncovers the rocks and sand. This is called low tide. Seashore animals have to **survive** in a habitat that is always changing.

STAY SAFE

- Be careful near the water, especially when the tide is in.
- When the tide goes out, wet rocks can be slippery.
- Never go into the sea on your own and make sure there are adults around to help if you need it.

9

Seashore zones

The highest place the water reaches is called the high tide line. In between the high tide line and the sea, the seashore is divided into different parts, called **zones**.

These seals rest in the splash zone. This is between the high tide line and the sea.

The different zones of a seashore

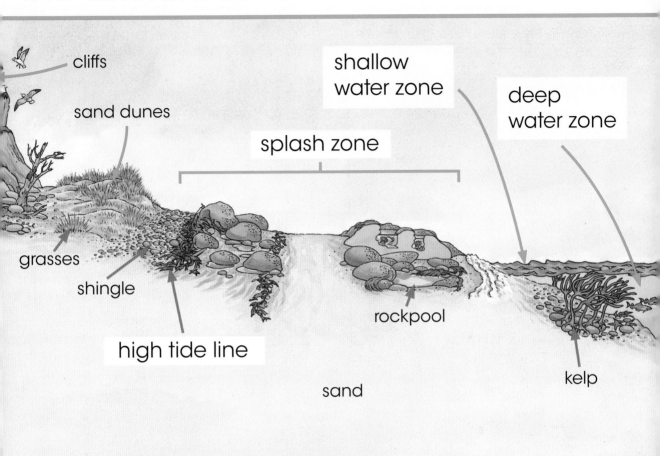

cliffs

sand dunes

shallow water zone

deep water zone

splash zone

grasses

shingle

high tide line

rockpool

sand

kelp

Different plants and animals live in the different zones. Some can live out of water for a long time. You find them higher up the shore. Others need to stay wet. They live lower down.

Exploring the seashore

Seashores are great places to explore. Look for plants and animals on and under the rocks, in rock pools, on the sand dunes, and at the water's edge.

Many animals hide away under the sand when the tide is out. This stops them drying out in the sun. But you can still search for clues, such as **tracks** and **casts**.

STAY SAFE

- Never disturb seashore animals or pull up plants.
- If you move shells or rocks to look under them, always put them back in the same place.
- Never try to move anemones or limpets.

What to take with you

- ✓ A fishing net
- ✓ A bucket
- ✓ A magnifying glass
- ✓ A fishing net
- ✓ A notebook and pencil
- ✓ Rubber-soled beach shoes or trainers

Seashore plants

bladderwrack

The best-known seashore plants are called seaweeds. You find them mostly on rocky seashores. They have special **features** to help them survive in their changing habitat.

Seaweeds have **holdfasts** instead of roots. These stick to rocks and stop the plants being washed away by the tides. Seaweeds also have tough leaves that do not get broken by the wind and waves.

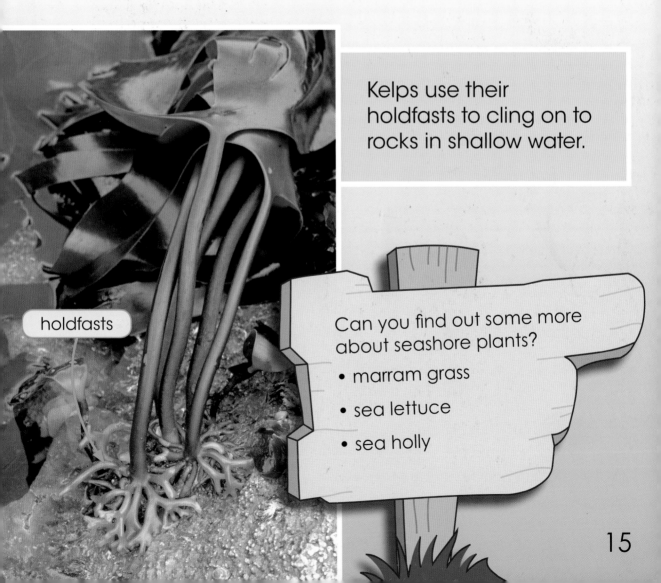

holdfasts

Kelps use their holdfasts to cling on to rocks in shallow water.

Can you find out some more about seashore plants?

- marram grass
- sea lettuce
- sea holly

In a rock pool

When the tide goes out, little pools of water are left behind in the rocks. They are called rock pools. Here you will see many different types of seashore creatures, hiding among the seaweed.

sea anemone

limpet

periwinkle

barnacle

When it is underwater, a sea anemone waves its **tentacles** to catch small creatures to eat. If the tides leave it high and dry, it pulls its tentacles in and looks like a blob of jelly.

Can you find out about the rock pool life above?
1 limpet
2 mussel
3 blenny (small fish)
4 goby
5 prawn
6 hermit crab
7 periwinkle
8 sea anemone

Under the sand

As the tide goes out, many seashore animals dig themselves into the sand. This means they escape from the hot sun and hide from hungry seabirds. They come out again when the tide comes back in.

green shore crab

whelk

razorshell

Some shells have one part. Others have two parts, joined together by a **hinge**. If you pick up a shell to look at, make sure sure that it is empty. You must never disturb live shells.

Seashore birds

Oystercatchers use their strong beaks to pull open mussel shells.

Many birds live and find food along the seashore. Some **soar** over the water or dive down to catch fish. Others use their beaks to dig around for shellfish and worms in the sand.

Look out for large groups of birds nesting on the cliffs above the beach. Kittiwakes build their nests from seaweed, stuck to the cliff with their droppings. Puffins nest in burrows on cliffs.

puffins

Can you find out some more about seashore birds?
- herring gull
- gannet
- plover

On the tide line

The best time to explore the tide line is when the tide is out. Look for dead seaweed, old crab shells, empty egg cases, and even jellyfish washed up on the seashore.

empty dogfish case

sandhopper

Tiny animals called sandhoppers jump about on the tide line. They are related to crabs and lobsters and are also called beach fleas. They feed on rotting seaweed.

Seashores in danger

Many of our seashores are in danger. Ships **accidentally** spill oil and the oil reaches the shore with the tide. People throw rubbish into the sea and on to the beach. This oil and rubbish can hurt seashore plants and animals.

This seabird has been covered in oil. It will need special cleaning.

You can help look after seashores by taking care when you visit them. You could go on a litter pick. Always go with an adult, and make sure you wear thick gloves. If you find broken glass or oily rubbish, ask an adult for help.

More things to do

There are a lot more things you can do on the seashore.

Looking at seashells

Collect some shells in your bucket. Make sure that they are empty. Sketch each shell in your notebook. Note down the shell's size, shape, and colour, and where you found it. Then put the shells back on the shore. You should not take shells or pebbles home.

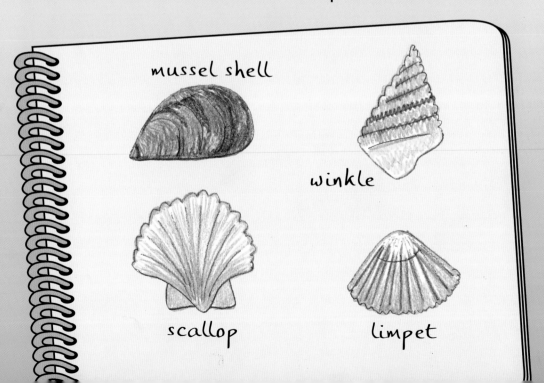

mussel shell

winkle

scallop

limpet

Seabird tally chart

Make a **tally chart** to keep count of the seabirds you spot. Use a bird identification book or print a guide off the Internet to help you recognize the birds. This chart shows some of the birds from this book but you can record different birds.

Bird	Number spotted
Puffins	I
Kittiwakes	III
Oystercatchers	II
Guillemots	ⱶⱶⱶⱶ I

kittiwake

oystercatcher

Ask an adult to help you look up these seabirds on the Internet.

Glossary

accidentally something that is not done on purpose

burrows holes under the ground used as homes by animals

casts coils of sand left on the shore by worms

features parts of a plant's or animal's body that helps it survive in its habitat

habitat place where animals and plants live

hinge something that joins two parts of an object, such a shell, together so that it can open and close

holdfast part of a seaweed that works like a root

molluscs animals with soft bodies, often protected by shells

sand dunes piles of sand blown by the wind

soar glide or fly in the air

survive be able to live

tally chart table that shows the number of something. A tally chart helps with counting.

tentacles long, thin parts of an animal's body, used for feeding, grasping, and moving

tides when the sea flows up on to the seashore, then out again, twice a day

tracks marks or patterns on the ground left by an animal

zones parts or sections

Find out more

Books to read

Seashore, Ken and Ron Preston-Mafham (Collins, 2004)

Usborne Spotter's Guides: The Seashore (Usborne Publishing, 2006)

Websites and organizations

Young People's Trust for the Environment
www.ypte.org.uk
This charity aims to encourage young people's understanding of the environment.

The Wildlife Trusts
www.wildlifetrusts.org
This is a voluntary organization that works to look after Britain's wildlife and habitats.

RNLI Beach safety
www.rnli.org.uk/what_we_do/sea_and_beach_safety
The RNLI website has lots of information to keep you safe on the beach.

Index